VERMONT

Text
Bill Harris

Captions
Ros Cocks

Photography
Fred M. Dole and Neil Sutherland

Design
Teddy Hartshorn

Commissioning Editor
Andrew Preston

Picture Editor
Annette Lerner

Editor
David Gibbon

Production
Ruth Arthur
Sally Connolly
Andrew Whitelaw

Director of Production
Gerald Hughes

CLB 2863
This 1992 edition published by Crescent Books,
distributed by Outlet Book Company, Inc., a Random House Company,
40 Engelhard Avenue, Avenel, New Jersey 07001.
Printed and bound in Singapore.
ISBN 0 517 07271 8
8 7 6 5 4 3 2 1

VERMONT

CRESCENT BOOKS
NEW YORK • AVENEL, NEW JERSEY

It was one of the great events of American history, but it also would have made a great comic opera.

It all began on a warm spring evening in 1775 at a tavern in Bennington, Vermont. Farmers who had just begun planting, and trappers who were getting ready to take to the woods for the season, had come together to share a few drinks and some gossip. A few weeks before that evening British redcoats had marched on Lexington, Massachusetts, and men like themselves were forced to defend their property. Vermont men understood what that meant. They had been defending their own property for almost a dozen years. The land they farmed had been granted to them, at a nice profit, by Governor Benning Wentworth of New Hampshire. But the King of England had granted the same territory to the Province of New York, and its governor was also making a profit selling it. If nothing else, it served to unite the people. They had already formed a civilian militia which they called the Green Mountain Boys, and it had a trusted leader named Ethan Allen.

Allen was among the men who were drinking rum diluted with hard cider that night in '75, and as the evening hours became morning hours he knew what he had to do. As he prepared to leave, he announced to the others that it was their patriotic duty to take Fort Ticonderoga for the Colonial cause.

This fort on the western side of Lake Champlain had been built by the French in 1755. Three years later its garrison of 4,000 men had no difficulty in turning back an English army of 15,000. The British took possession after the treaty of Paris in 1763, but because of lack of money they let it deteriorate. Its garrison had been reduced to less than 100 men, but its two dozen cannon were in good shape and there was plenty of powder behind its walls. Allen could be forgiven if he changed his mind in the cold light of dawn.

But there were other forces at work. A Connecticut apothecary named Benedict Arnold put on a fancy, gold-braided military uniform and started riding toward Boston as soon as he heard the news of the skirmish at Lexington. He had come up with same idea, and in a few weeks had an official commission as a colonel in the militia, and a mission to bring back the Ticonderoga cannon. Meanwhile, the Hartford Committee of Correspondence appropriated £300 and sent eight men on the same mission.

The Connecticut group, along with about fifty recruits picked up along the way, arrived in Bennington first. Ethan Allen had already begun rounding up his Green Mountain Boys and he had come up with a plan. They moved on together toward Castleton to put them within easy striking distance of the fort and then held a council of war. Allen was put in command.

His first move was to send one of the scruffiest of his men to the fort, where he posed as a trapper in need of a shave and a haircut. The British had no reason to doubt his story and he came away with more than a new image. He confirmed that there were no more than 50 soldiers inside and he noted that there was a gaping hole in the fort's southern wall. He also reported that the defenders seemed to have no idea that they were about to be attacked.

Allen, meanwhile, had dispatched two small parties to steal enough boats to allow them to attack from the water. The boats and his 230 men were to meet in a cove just out of sight of Ticonderoga. While the men were waiting for the boats to arrive, Colonel Benedict Arnold and his valet rode into camp. He had a document issued by the Massachusetts Committee of Safety that named him commander of the Ticonderoga attack force.

Allen had a few choice words to offer about that, all of which added up to a refusal to give up his command. His men backed him and told Arnold that they'd go back home before they'd follow him into battle. But Benedict Arnold wasn't the sort of man to be bullied any more than Ethan Allen was, and it was finally agreed that Arnold could march next to Allen.

They almost didn't march at all. Only two boats arrived and they weren't able to ferry more than 48 men with limited supplies across the lake before the light of day would ruin their surprise. Allen decided to take a chance.

At four o'clock on the morning of May 10, 1775, the tiny company of untrained men, each of whom had armed himself, landed under the ramparts of Fort Ticonderoga and marched single file to the south side, where the breach in the wall would help them make their dramatic entrance. There was one guard stationed there. He raised his rifle and aimed it straight at Ethan Allen. It misfired. Then he lunged with his bayonet, but the commander of the Green Mountain Boys knocked him unconscious.

Allen's men followed him inside on the run. There was no need for silence any longer and they were all yelling like wild Indians. The ruckus woke the lieutenant who was second in command. He appeared at the door of his quarters without his trousers. But not without his dignity. "By what authority have you entered His Majesty's fort?" he asked. Allen is said to have replied, "In the name of the Great Jehovah and the Continental Congress!"

The lieutenant was not impressed by that or anything else Ethan Allen might have to say, but all those howling ruffians behind him must have made an impression. He began to stall for time, but Allen would have none of it. He waved his sword over his head and announced that he was taking possession of the fort and everything in it. His men, meanwhile, were putting teeth into his words. They hadn't actually harmed anyone yet, but they made it clear to the soldiers that they were ready to kill every last one of them and have fun doing it. The fort's commander had managed to get into his uniform by then and when he appeared on the parade ground he was taken prisoner immediately. Most of his men were already prisoners in their own beds.

By the time the sun came up that morning Fort Ticonderoga had fallen. No one on either side had been killed. No one had even been wounded.

In an hour or two all of the Green Mountain Boys had been ferried across the lake. But there wasn't much left for them to do. Thirty-eight British soldiers, a captain and two lieutenants had been taken prisoner, along with twenty-four women and children. Allen dispatched about fifty of his men to Crown Point, a smaller British fort a few miles north. The facility wasn't much more than a ruin, and the soldiers at Crown Point also surrendered without firing a shot. It yielded one sergeant and eight privates for the prisoner list. It also added to the impressive list of captured material. In addition to boats and food supplies, the two raids yielded more than 200 artillery pieces, about half of which were ready to fire.

Some of the Green Mountain Boys who took Ticonderoga fired a salute with one of the cannon that fateful morning. Legend says that the blast was so loud it nearly woke up their fellow militiamen down in the wine cellar.

Among the booty they found in the fort was ninety gallons of the best quality rum these men had ever seen. It wasn't there when the sun went down. Ethan Allen had his share of it, of course, but he spent much of the day dealing with more important matters. He

wrote letters to the Continental Congress and the governments of New York and Massachusetts. He ordered the prisoners sent to Connecticut with the hope "they may serve as ransom for our friends in Boston." He also took time gratefully to receive a commission from the Committee of War. Now he was just as much a Colonel as Benedict Arnold.

Each of Allen's letters mentioned that Arnold had been at his side, but the message was clear where credit was due. Some historians claim that the Allen correspondence was an act of hubris, and they have plenty of examples to back up the claim. But the event was certainly an act of bravery. The capture of two of His Majesty's forts was a terrific morale booster for the Colonies. The skirmishes that had taken place in Massachusetts in April were easily interpreted as defensive on the part of the Minutemen. That definition didn't apply to Ticonderoga and Crown Point. The Colonies had not declared war on England and the Green Mountain Boys had left themselves wide open to charges of treason. They ran the risk of hanging.

The Colonies, meanwhile, were in a quandary about what to do with the forts and all those supplies that had been delivered into their laps. The Governor of New York refused to admit he had received Allen's letter. Massachusetts and Connecticut, both of which had approved the action in advance, turned the matter over to the Continental Congress, which in turn wished the Great Jehovah would lift the burden from its shoulders.

Congress responded by accepting responsibility for the forts, though not for the act of capturing them. It stretched its collective imagination to the point of saying that Allen and his men had taken defensive action, and ordered that the captured supplies should be held in safekeeping until "the restoration of the former harmony between Great Britain and these colonies, so ardently wished-for by the latter." The Connecticut Committee of War paid for the 90 gallons of rum.

Allen later mounted a letter-writing campaign that convinced Congress of the error of its ways. The forts were not disarmed and the surplus cannon were sent to Boston, where they were eventually put to good use. Meanwhile, Ethan Allen had other fish to fry.

He managed to get Congressional approval for the creation of an official regiment of Green Mountain Boys, which would serve under and be paid by New York. But when the force was formed and its officers chosen, Ethan Allen's name was nowhere on the list. It was cruel blow to the man who had led the Boys against the New Yorkers for five years and who had showed them the taste of glory at Ticonderoga. But if Ethan Allen had been accused of being arrogant, overbearing and vain, he didn't lack grace. He was quick to support the officers the town committees had chosen. They were still his friends, after all. They requested that General Schuyler, their commanding officer, allow Allen to accompany them as a civilian scout. The request was granted after the general extracted a promise from Allen that he would behave himself. Some promises, though, are hard to keep.

They put Allen to work to soften up the attitude of the Canadians and the Indians in advance of making an attack on the British forces north of the border. He had a gift for such things, and before the attempt was made Indians in every Canadian tribe said they were proud to call themselves "Yankees." As the campaign got under way, Allen went behind the lines to recruit more converts. In his travels he met another scout like himself who said he had two hundred recruits following him. Allen himself had about one hundred and that gave him an idea. That night the two men hatched a scheme to attack Montreal.

It didn't matter to them that there were more than six thousand people there compared to their three hundred. Allen had it on good authority that there weren't more than sixty British soldiers among them, and he'd never met a Canadian who didn't like him. They decided to meet at dawn the next day and attack immediately. But when dawn came the larger of the two little armies was still bogged down on the banks of the St. Lawrence. Allen and his hundred men were at the gates of the city on an island in the middle of the river. They couldn't turn and run for the same reason their reinforcements couldn't reach them. It was mid-afternoon before the Canadians realized what a puny force was at their door, and by then it was all over for Ethan Allen. Later that afternoon he was in chains in the hold of a British schooner on its way to England, where it was promised he would hang.

A great many officials in the Colonies breathed a sigh of relief; Allen's attack had ruined any possibility of a confederation with Canada and gave the British a propaganda victory that outweighed the benefits of his adventure at Ticonderoga. But when Allen arrived in England, the British realized they were saddled with a very thorny problem. There was no doubt in their minds that the man deserved to be hanged for treason. But he was a British subject, entitled to a trial by a jury of his peers. They could call him a prisoner of war, but then they couldn't hang him, and it would amount to a public admission that a war was actually going on. In London they preferred to regard it as an isolated uprising. They settled the problem by putting Allen on a ship bound for America. He got his freedom when he was exchanged for a British officer in 1778. The first person he went to see was General George Washington, who had to admit "there is an original something in him that commands admiration."

Allen went back to Vermont after that. During the three years he had been away, his home territory, which had been known as the New Hampshire Grants, had declared itself the independent Republic of Vermont. It had its own constitution, the first in North America with voting rights for every man whether he was a property owner or not, and the first to make slavery illegal. Ethan Allen wasn't one of its founders, but his spirit was well served, and the new constitution promised good things for this man who owned more than 12,000 acres in the Republic.

The Revolution would drag on for three more years, but Ethan Allen wasn't an active participant. He wasn't an active participant in governing the Republic of Vermont, either. But he knew instinctively how to pull the right strings and his influence was felt everywhere. He extended his influence beyond its borders by writing a book with the very long title: *A Narrative of Colonel Allen's Captivity, Containing His Voyages and Travels, With the Most Remarkable Occurrences Respecting Him and Many Other Continental Prisoners of Different Ranks and Characters. Interspersed With Some Political Observations. Written by Himself and Now Published for the Information of the Curious in all Nations.*

It aroused the curiosity of enough readers to sell out three printings. Over the next few years it was reprinted nineteen times. It made Ethan Allen's place in the history of America as secure as it was in the Republic of Vermont.

He continued to fight against New York's claims to territory in the Republic which delayed the hope that Vermont might become a state under the new Constitution. The matter was finally settled peacefully when Vermont paid New York for her claims, and the Green Mountain State was admitted to the Union on March 4, 1791. Many called it the first child of the thirteen colonies. But it was a contrary child.

Ethan Allen may have been the contrariest of all our Colonial heroes, but Vermonters have always taken special pride in following in his footsteps. And the tradition doesn't apply just to people. In the 1780s a Vermont teacher named Justin Morgan began making his rounds in a carriage pulled by a horse the like of which no one in the world had ever seen before. It had a lean face with a broad forehead. Its neck was short, as was its back, and its legs muscular. It was sure-footed and walked fast. It could run short distances faster than any horse in the Republic of Vermont. And it was as gentle as it was strong. Morgan never said how he had developed this wonderful new animal, but the original horse lived for 29 years and passed its characteristics to enough offspring to create an entire new breed. Its uncommon strength and endurance made it the animal of choice for railroads and stagecoach lines. Its sure-footedness and speed made it perfect as a cavalry horse. But the origin of the first Morgan horse, which just suddenly appeared one day, is one of the secrets locked away in the Green Mountains.

Vermonters often appear secretive to outsiders. Calvin Coolidge seemed to confirm it when he went to the White House and made it a point not to volunteer any information unless somebody went to the trouble to ask. But the key is in the asking. They're actually quite generous with their ideas and most of those ideas are completely original. William Lloyd Garrison became the first voice for the abolition of slavery in America, decades after it was outlawed in Vermont, with a newspaper he published in Bennington. Stephen Douglas took the message west from Vermont to Illinois, where he bested Abraham Lincoln in a race for the United States Senate.

Horace Greeley, who was credited with advising young men to migrate west, himself migrated from Vermont to New York to seek his fortune. But he said of his former neighbors in Poultney, "I have never since known a community so generally moral, intelligent, industrious or friendly."

Consider what their intelligence and industry have given us: Elisha Graves Otis of Halifax perfected the elevator; Edwin Drake of Castleton drilled the first oil well; Jim Fisk of Brattleboro built the Erie Railroad; Richard Morris Hunt of Brattleboro designed the base for the Statue of Liberty, among other architectural treasures; and Brigham Young of Whitingham, following the teachings of Sharon's Joseph Smith, led the Mormons west. The first troop of Boy Scouts in America earned its Tenderfoot badge in Barre. And the magazine *American Heritage* was, appropriately, first published in Vermont.

A name almost lost to American history, though it shouldn't be, is H. Nelson Jackson, who set out from Vermont in 1903 in a brand-new Winton automobile bound for San Francisco, California. No one had ever crossed the continent in a car, but Jackson had bet $50 it could be done. He won the bet. When he got to California, he turned around and headed back. The round trip took two months and nine days. Along the way, someone asked him where he was from. When he was told, he said, "What in hell will you Vermonters do next?" What indeed?

Robert Frost once said that Vermont is "a state in a very natural state." Vermont people work hard to keep it that way. He also warned that "New York is seeping up this way." But if they welcome paying guests to their ski slopes and share their maple sugar with folks who come to admire their hills and valleys, Vermonters don't show any sign of adopting the strangers' ways. More often than not it's the opposite that happens. To paraphrase General Washington, there is an original something in them that commands admiration.

Facing page: pumpkins and brilliantly colored foliage make Groton, and five other villages in northeast Vermont, famous for the Northeast Kingdom Foliage Festival. This lasts a week and incorporates church breakfasts, house tours and craft fairs. The other villages taking part are Barnet, Cabot, Peacham, Plainfield and Walden.

Facing page: Hyde Park (top), northern Vermont, near St. Johnsbury on the Passumpsic River. Above and below: Metcalf Pond, north of Jeffersonville. Top right: Chimney Point, Lake Champlain. Maple sap, collected in buckets from the tree trunk, is reduced to syrup in sugar houses (right). Bottom right: Fairfax Falls, northeast of Burlington. Overleaf: fall scenery near West Burke.

These pages and overleaf: the Green Mountains of northwest Vermont. Mount Mansfield (above, below and overleaf) is Vermont's highest peak at 4393 feet. Stowe (left and facing page) is the area's principal resort, offering a long winter-sporting season with a good variety of ski trails which connect Mount Mansfield to Spruce Peak (3320 feet). In summer Stowe is also a popular center for hiking and climbing.

These pages: the stunning phenomenon of the Vermont fall. This is at its most spectacular in the "Northeast Kingdom." Starting in late August and reaching a climax in mid-September, the fiery maple leaves are one of this state's great tourist attractions. These trees are also the source of maple syrup for which sap is collected and boiled down. Thirty gallons of sap reduce to one gallon of syrup. Overleaf: farmland south of Burlington.

MONTREAL
110 MILES.
NEW YORK
292 MILES.
SHELBURNE
ST. ALBANS
40 MILES.
RUTLAND
60 MILES.
RAILWAY EXPRESS AGENCY
C.A.F.

Exhibits at Shelburne Museum Park (above) include a railway depot (facing page), general store (below), lighthouse (right), and the SS Ticonderoga (bottom right), a side-wheeler steamboat. This collection of Americana was initiated by a railroad magnate a hundred years ago. It lies eight miles south of Burlington (top right), the fashionable playground city on Lake Champlain (overleaf).

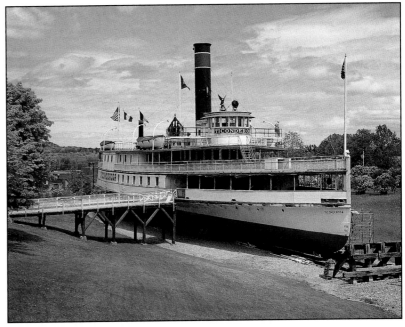

Facing page: Otter Creek rapids near Bristol. Above: Waitesfield Federated Church. Below: Williston Church, near Burlington. Top right: Mad River, near Waitsfield. Right: typical red-barned farm near Waterbury. The Rock of Ages granite quarry at Graniteville (bottom right), Barre, has been in operation since 1812 and now produces one third of the nation's memorial stones.

COURT HOUSE

33

In late summer the maples begin to shine out from among the evergreens, splashing the landscape with vivid color. St. Johnsbury (below) is famous for its maple syrup production and the Fairbanks Museum of Natural Science and Planetarium. Left: the satellite villages of St. Johnsbury, namely Danville (top), West Danville (center), on Joe's Pond, and Peacham (bottom).

Tunbridge (facing page and top right), south of Barre, with its pretty Methodist Church, holds a popular "World's Fair" in September. Above: church in Strafford, a prosperous town east of Tunbridge. Below: Peacham, good for cross-country skiing in winter. Right: Barnet, on the Connecticut River. Waits River (bottom right) is in central Vermont close to East Topsham (overleaf) nestling in its pastoral bowl.

These pages: Plymouth Notch, Plymouth homestead of Calvin Coolidge, is open to the public May through October. This is where the USA's thirtieth president was living when he was sworn into office in 1923. The Bible still lies on his open desk (below). Overleaf: Pomfret, a typical Vermont hamlet.

Grafton (above left, left, below left, below and facing page bottom) once prospered on woolen cloth production and soapstone mining. The pretty nineteenth-century town decayed, but was restored in the 1960s by Hall and Dean Mathey. Above: Bennington Battle Monument. Green Mountain National Forest acts as a backdrop to the Athens (facing page top) and Newfane (overleaf) regions.